How To Survive A Marriage
with a Non-Christian Spouse

BY: SHARON LEE GRAHAM, D.C. Coun., Th.D

McClure™ publishing

McClure Publishing, Inc.
Bloomingdale, IL

Copyright © 2012

Pastor Sharon Lee Graham, D.C.Coun., Th.D for McClure Publishing, Inc.

How to Survive a Marriage with a Non-Christian Spouse

All rights reserved. Printed and bound in the United States of America. According to the 1976 United States Copyright Act, no part of this book may be reproduced or utilized in any form or by any means, electronic or mechanical, including photocopying, recording, or by any information storage or retrieval system, except by a reviewer who may quote brief passages in a review to be printed in a magazine or newspaper, without permission in writing from the Publisher: Inquiries should be addressed to McClure Publishing, Inc. Permissions Department, 358 West Army Trail Road, #205, Bloomingdale, Illinois 60108. First Printing: June 4, 2012.

King James Version: Scripture quotations marked "KJV" are taken from the Holy Bible, King James Version, Cambridge, 1769.

"Scripture taken from THE AMPLIFIED BIBLE. Old Testament copyright (c) 1965, 1987 by The Zondervan Corporation. The Amplified New Testament copyright (c) 1958, 1987 by The Lockman Foundation. Used by permission."

Quotations and/or reprints in excess of one thousand (1,000) verses, or other permission requests, must be directed and approved in writing by Zondervan Bible Publishers (Amp. O.T.), or The Lockman Foundation (Amp. N.T.).

The author and publisher have made every effort to ensure the accuracy and completeness of information contained in this book, we assume no responsibility for errors, inaccuracies, omissions, or any inconsistency therein.

Any slights of people, places, belief systems or organizations are unintentional. Any resemblance to anyone living, dead or somewhere in between is truly coincidental.

ISBN-13: 978-0-9833697-3-8

ISBN-10: 0-9833697-3-9

LCCN: 2012942145

Book cover illustration taken from 123rf.com – creative images.

Cover Design and Interior Layout by Kathy McClure
www.mcclurepublishing.com

To order additional copies, please contact
McClure Publishing, Inc.
800.659.4908

CONTENTS

Page

INTRODUCTION

CHAPTER I - THE WEDDING VOWS 11

CHAPTER II - NOW THAT YOU ARE MARRIED 19

CHAPTER III - HOW TO SURVIVE 39

CHAPTER IV - TO THE SINGLES 61

CHAPTER V - CONCLUSION 69

NOTES AND COMMENT

About the Author

ACKNOWLEDGMENTS

I give special thanks to my children, M. Yvette (Graham) Williams, Mary Y. Graham, J. R. Graham, Jr., and Angelica S. Graham (granddaughter), for enduring the days of my youth.

I extend appreciation to J. R. Graham, Sr., for pushing me and causing me to stretch into the mature place I am today.

I shall forever love and appreciate my father, Raymond Boyd, my mother, Martha Boyd, and my grandmother, Alma Bridgewater, for teaching me to be responsible and respectful.

To my best friend, Betty Parker and James Parker, thank you for praying for me, believing in me, and for standing with me during one of the most difficult times of my life.

To Annette Brown, Rhoda and Bill Barrett, Linda and Jerome Parker, and Sandra and Hubert Reynolds thank you for supporting me and believing in me.

I am grateful to the youth and to all of the members and partners of Life In Christ~Christ In Me Ministries, Inc., for all of the support and prayers that have helped make this book possible. Most of all I thank my Lord and Savior, Jesus Christ, for loving me and for calling me for such a time as this. He is worthy of all glory, honor, power and praise. Without Him I could do nothing.

INTRODUCTION

This book is written for the benefit of both male and female Christians who are married to non-Christian spouses. When God created Adam and Eve and united them as husband and wife, he blessed them. He put his approval upon them and told them to be fruitful, multiply, replenish the earth and subdue it. God's plan for them was a good plan, not an evil one. The word "blessed" means to be happy. God intended for Adam and Eve to be happy, and they were until a third party stepped in. The Word of God tells us that we are not to allow man to separate what God has joined together. There are so many cases today where not only a third party has stepped in, but a multitude of intruders have stepped into the picture and have wreaked havoc into the unions that God has joined.

The forces of the evil one have a different plan for marriage. Their plan is perverse and is orchestrated by Satan, the evil one. The forces of the evil one are the fallen angels. Their plan is contrary to God's plan and is designed to bring sorrow and pain to the marriage.

Adam and Eve would have been blessed in their union, and not brought under the curse, if only they had walked in total obedience to the command of the Lord God Almighty. Because of their disobedience, all mankind was born under the same curse.

We can thank God for the blood of Jesus that washes away our sins, and for the gospel of Jesus Christ, which is the power of God that brings salvation, healing, and deliverance. For those who are wondering how they got into such a mess of a so-called marriage and can hardly wait for a chance to be single again, after reading this book, my prayer is that the saving, healing, and delivering power of God will sweep over your life as never before. Being single again will not solve the problem; only Jesus can solve the problem and make you every whit whole.

For those who are in the marriage for the duration, may the Lord anoint you with enduring power from above as you read the words of wisdom contained herein.

For the singles that might be afraid to marry after witnessing some of the worst marriages of this age, do not choose to remain single or turn to some perverse lifestyle in an effort to avoid the horrors that you have witnessed. This book will help you avoid some of the common pitfalls made by others. There are still good marriages today. There are many happy couples that have learned to put God first in their marriage.

Before entering into a relationship, it is important that the parties involved be made aware of the differences between the Christian and non-Christian lifestyles, and the consequences of being unequally yoked. Godly counsel before marriage is of the utmost importance. You will be able to see the differences between the marriages of those who receive premarital counseling and those who reject it.

May the Lord richly bless and enlighten you as you read. May you be enriched by the hindsight of others, which is always 20/20.

How To Survive A Marriage
With A Non-Christian Spouse

CHAPTER I

THE WEDDING VOWS

DEARLY beloved: We are gathered together here in the sight of God, and in the face of this company, to join together this Man and this Woman in holy matrimony; which is commended of St. Paul to be honorable among all men: and therefore is not by any to be entered into unadvisedly or lightly; but reverently, discreetly, advisedly, and in the fear of God. Into this holy estate, these two persons present come now to be joined. If any man can show just cause why they may not lawfully be joined together, let him now speak, or else hereafter forever hold his peace.[1]

---

[1] Hiscox, Edward T. The Star Book For Ministers: Revised Edition: Judson Press, Pennsylvania, 1968.

Maybe you have encountered at least one person who said they wished someone had spoken out and objected to their marriage. If you are married, have you ever wished that someone had spoken out and objected to marriage right in the middle of the ceremony? Probably not, at least not on the day of the wedding; but as the years passed, I am sure someone has thought back to the day of the wedding and asked, "why didn't someone stop me from making the biggest mistake of my life?" Since no one stopped you, the wedding continued and so did the vows.

> I REQUIRE and charge you both, as ye will answer at the dreadful day of judgment, when the secrets of all hearts shall be disclosed, that if either of you know any impediment why ye may not be lawfully joined together in matrimony, ye do now confess it. For be ye well assured, that if any persons are joined together otherwise than as God's word doth allow, their marriage is not lawful.
>
> WILT thou have this Woman to thy wedded wife, to live together after God's ordinance, in the holy estate of matrimony? Wilt thou love her, comfort her, honor, and keep her, in sickness and in health; and, forsaking all

others, keep thee only unto her, so long as ye both shall live?

WILT thou have this Man to thy wedded husband, to live together after God's ordinance, in the holy estate of matrimony? Wilt thou obey him and serve him, love, honor, and keep him, in sickness and in health; and, forsaking all others, keep thee only unto him, so long as ye both shall live?

Next, someone gives the bride away and the exchange of vows take place. Each promises the other that they will have, hold, love, cherish, obey, forsake all others, and will keep themselves for each other only, whether things get better or worse, whether their health fails or remains, whether they have their riches or lose them, they promise to only allow death to do the parting of them. A most sacred ceremony has been performed before man and God. Serious vows have been made while heaven and earth witness.

Wedding vows are made to each other, in the presence of man and God, and should not be taken lightly. The breaking of a vow is to be viewed seriously. The consequence of breaking a vow can be severe enough to cause the loss of one's natural life and their eternal soul. It is not Christ-like to take the heart and emotions of another and knowingly deceive them with false hope. When vows are exchanged, it is assumed that each party has the intention of keeping the vows, whatever the cost. The person on the receiving end of the vow has trust and is in expectancy of receiving nothing less than what has been vowed.

"Better is it that thou shouldest not vow, than that thou shouldest vow and not pay."[2] Vows should be made only after careful and prayerful consideration and godly counsel. Rash promises should be avoided. Never allow yourself to be put into a position of pressure from others that would cause you to make vows that you cannot keep.

Each person who makes a vow is expected to keep the vow. I have heard conversations concerning problems encountered between marriages of Christians to non-Christians. Most of these conversations tend to lean toward non-Christian spouses who expect the Christian spouse to keep their part of the vows, and to bend over backwards while doing so. There is a name for this way of

---
[2] KJV, Ecclesiastes 5:5

thinking, it is what we call a "double standard." How would you like to be told what you had better not do, and the person prohibiting you does the very thing you were just prohibited from doing? When you question them, you are told you are being prohibited because you are a Christian, but they did it because they are not a Christian. How would you endure a relationship loaded with double standards? Would it be like living in bondage? Do you think things will get better after a while? Do you think you can change a person? How do you feel about double standards? Before marriage, someone might think it's cute, but after marriage, you might feel differently. A Christian's standard is to be different from a non-Christian's standard.

> Now we have received, not the spirit of the world, but the spirit which is of God; that we might know the things that are freely given to us of God. Which things also we speak, not in the words which man's wisdom teacheth, but which the Holy Ghost teacheth; comparing spiritual things with spiritual. But the natural man receiveth not the things of the Spirit of God: for they are foolishness unto him: neither

can he know them, because they are spiritually discerned.[3]

God is so much smarter than we are. He has given us his Spirit to teach us so that we might know the things that he has so freely given to us. The Christian has the Spirit of God, and should seek God for discernment. The non-Christian does not have the Spirit of God and, therefore, cannot live up to the requirements of God. Remember, God's standards and ways are spiritual and are spiritually discerned by those who are walking after the Spirit of God. To the non-Christian, God's standards and ways are foolishness. The non-Christian, lacking the power of the Holy Ghost, is unable to receive God's standards to live by; therefore, the non-Christian is unable to discern and apply spiritual standards God's way. They tend to exclude themselves from these high standards by using the excuse of not being a Christian. In other words, in their mind, only the Christians have to keep their parts of the marriage vows.

"An ungodly man diggeth up evil: and in his lips there is as a burning fire."[4] Who, in their right mind,

---

[3] KJV, I Corinthians 2:12-14

would want to exchange wedding vows with an ungodly man or an ungodly woman? "Can two walk together, except they be agreed?"[5] One spouse has the power of the True and Living God that enables them to make vows and to keep them, while the other spouse does not have the power of God and will not be able to be the godly spouse God has intended for them to be. This calls for an unbalanced and unhappy union. There are Christians who have already made their vows in holy matrimony to non-Christians. They suffer the consequences of disobeying God's word. There are Christians who married in the faith, but later on in the marriage their Christian spouse left the faith; nevertheless, God is still holding both spouses accountable for keeping the vows that were made. Even if one spouse breaks the wedding vows, this does not give the other spouse license to do the same.

If you are loyal and believe firmly in commitment, you should seek the same loyalty and commitment from the person with whom you wish to exchange wedding vows. Do not settle for less. If the person with whom you

---

[4] KJV, Proverbs 16:27
[5] KJV, Amos 3:3

are dating is unfaithful and uncommitted to God, will they be unfaithful and uncommitted to the wedding vows? Anyone can make a vow, but it takes the strength of the Lord to keep it.

Finally, get counseling and give thought before you exchange vows with anyone who is of an opposing faith. There was an event concerning a couple having opposing faiths. They married, had a child and that was when the trouble manifested. Divorce and a court appearance all because one parent did not want the child to be baptized as a member of the other parent's place of worship.

CHAPTER II

NOW THAT YOU ARE MARRIED

Being united in holy matrimony is one of the most wonderful events that could possibly happen on earth. It is an event created by God and longed for by mankind.

> And God said, Let us make man in our image, after our likeness: and let them have dominion over the fish of the sea, and over the fowl of the air, and over the cattle, and over all the earth, and over every creeping thing that creepth upon the earth. So God created man in his own image, in the image of God created he him; male and female created he them. And God blessed them, and God said unto them, Be fruitful, and multiply, and replenish the earth, and subdue it: and have dominion over the fish of the sea, and over the fowl of the air, and

over every living thing that moveth upon the earth.[1]

And the Lord God said, It is not good that the man should be alone; I will make him a help meet for him. And out of the ground the Lord God formed every beast of the field, and every fowl of the air; and brought them unto Adam to see what he would call them: and whatsoever Adam called every living creature, that was the name thereof. And Adam gave the names to all cattle, and to the fowl of the air, and to every beast of the field; but for Adam there was not found a help meet for him. And the Lord God caused a deep sleep to fall upon Adam, and he slept: and he took one of his ribs, and closed up the flesh instead thereof; And the rib, which the Lord God had taken from man, made he a woman, and brought her unto the man. And Adam said, This is now bone of my bones, and flesh of my flesh: she shall be called Woman, because she was taken out of Man. Therefore shall a man leave his father and his mother, and shall cleave unto his wife: and they shall be one flesh. And they were both naked, the man and his wife, and were not ashamed.[2]

There are instances where some will choose not to marry, and that is fine. It is not a sin to be single. Jesus

---

[1] KJV, Genesis 1:26-28
[2] KJV, Genesis 2:18-25

said, "For there are some eunuchs, which were so born from their mother's womb: and there are some eunuchs, which were made eunuchs of men: and there be eunuchs, which have made themselves eunuchs for the Kingdom of Heaven's sake. He that is able to receive it, let him receive it."[3] Jesus knew that all men would not be able to receive the lifestyle of not being married.

For those who are destined to marry, God has said that it is not good for man to be alone. There were many animals and creeping things in the Garden of Eden, but none of them were designed to meet Adam's needs. God knows the needs of mankind and has always been wise enough to meet those needs; let us not forget it. God caused a deep sleep to fall upon Adam. While Adam slept, God took one of Adam's ribs and made Adam the help meet that was compatible for him. Adam woke up and was presented with a wife designed by God. Adam would never have to be alone again. From the beginning, God designed the husband and wife to be one flesh, to leave mother and father, and to cleave to one another. This is a

---

[3] KJV, Matthew 19:12

biblical principle. Whenever this principle is broken, look for serious trouble on the horizon. In other words, the umbilical cord and the apron string must be cut.

There is a time and a place for all things. There may be times when married people portray the behavior of the fetus but, the fact is, they are adults. They have taken on the role of being married and are held accountable as being adults. To all of the parents who feel they have failed to convey the proper nourishment to their fetus, it is too late and impossible to reconnect the umbilical cord after marriage. You can repent and ask God for forgiveness for your lack of properly teaching your child the way that God would have him or her to go; but after they marry, you must let them go. This is not to say that you cannot give advice if asked; however, you must be cautious, wise, understanding, and unbiased. If you have problems being any of these, keep your mouth closed and open it only when it is time to pray. Even if you, as a parent, were not properly taught and did not learn the ways of God until later in life, you can still repent and obtain forgiveness and mercy for yourself and your adult child. You can pray for godly wisdom and for God's divine intervention on behalf of your child's marriage. The principle of cutting the umbilical cord not only applies to both the man and to the woman, but to the parents also. Some parents have matured enough to graciously allow the cutting to take place, while there are others who have not. Some pretend to be sick or try to place guilt trips on their adult children in order to hold on.

The husband and wife must guard their marriage against those who might try using these tactics. Beware of the parents who play one spouse against the other, or who make negative comments that insinuate that the one is not good enough for the other. Most parents mean well, but sometimes they have a difficult time of discerning when to stay out of their children's, who happen to be adults, marriages. Couples must never allow anyone or anything to cause division in their marriage. "Wherefore they are no more twain, but one flesh. What therefore God hath joined together, let not man put asunder."[4]

---

[4] KJV, Matthew 19:6

There are those spouses who refuse to let go of the apron string. They hold on to the last thread of the apron, as they scream, cry, and throw temper tantrums. They expect their spouse to conform to the way things were done at home. To cook like mama cooked or to whistle like daddy whistled. They want the same type of furniture that mom and dad had, and they want the house painted the same color as their mom's and dad's house. They want their spouse to dress, walk and talk like mom and dad. These requirements are indicators of a person who has very little sensitivity for the pain that this type of behavior inflicts upon their spouse. These requirements make the spouse feel inadequate for not being a clone of their spouse's parents. "Be sober, be vigilant; because your adversary the devil, as a roaring lion, walketh about, seeking whom he may devour:"[5] Husbands and wives are to be mindful, considerate, wise and alert concerning the schemes Satan tries to slip into marriages. Satan eases his way in through the smallest situations. He is seeking whom he may devour. Satan is waiting for permission to destroy marriages. He hates for families to be united

---

[5] KJV, I Peter 5:8

together in the power of God because this kind of unity defeats him every time. He awaits for the possibility of a breakdown in the marriage so that he can launch his wicked attacks. The scriptures explain the importance and power that lie in unity. When the husband and wife fight against each other, they are fighting against their own flesh. When they were united in holy matrimony, they became one flesh.

> And Jesus knew their thoughts, and said unto them, Every kingdom divided against itself is brought to desolation; and every city or house divided against itself shall not stand: And if Satan cast out Satan, he is divided against himself; how shall then his kingdom stand? And if I by Beelzebub cast out devils, by whom do your children cast them out? Therefore they shall be your judges.[6]

> There is one alone, and there is not a second; yea, he hath neither child nor brother: yet is there no end of all his labor; neither is his eye satisfied with riches; neither saith he, For whom do I labor, and bereave my soul of good? This is also vanity, yea, it is a sore travail. Two are better than one; because they have good reward for their labor. For if they fall, the one will lift up his fellow: but woe to him that is alone when he falleth; for he hath

---

[6] KJV, Matthew 12:25-27

not another to help him up. Again, if two lie together, then they have heat: but how can one be warm alone? And if one prevail against him, two shall withstand him; and a threefold cord is not quickly broken.[7]

It is vitally important for husbands and wives to be on one accord and to serve the same Lord. As the scripture has so plainly stated concerning Satan's house, that if Satan's house is divided against itself, it shall not stand; the same goes for Christian spouses who are divided against each other. No one is exempt from obeying the scriptures. This principle is applied to everyone. For those Christians who have chosen to marry non-Christians, there is a price to pay. The house is divided, it is going to take God's grace, and much work has to be done in order for the Christian spouse to stand.

There is much sorrow, grief, betrayal, loneliness, anger, bitterness, shame, regret, and the list goes on, when Christians marry non-Christians. Much repentance, forgiveness, prayer, fasting, and standing on the Word of God has to be done if healing is desired in this marital situation. Someone said words to the effect that if you

---

[7] KJV, Ecclesiastes 4:8-12

make your bed hard, you must lie in it. Another person said words to the effect that if you make your bed hard you will roll over in it more often. Nevertheless, I say take heed to how you make your bed because you must lie in the bed you make.

Marriage is an investment. No one should be willing to invest their heart, soul and body into the life of someone who would only bring pain and regrets as the return. When you give your heart to someone in marriage, you want that someone to be caring, kind, loving, and gentle with you. You expect great returns; in fact, your expectations probably exceed what is reasonable. Marriages take time and effort. When there is no investment of time and effort, there will be no gain, but rather the door is opened for loss to take place. The Christian spouse has invested time in the Word of God, prayer, fasting, and fellowship with believers. Christians invest their time and talent for charitable causes. They visit the sick and help the widows and fatherless; whereas, non-Christians do not share in all of these kinds of investments. There are some non-Christians who do charitable work and who are good helpers and have a giving heart. Do not be fooled by these kinds of non-Christians. They are called non-Christians because God is not first in their lives, they do not love God, nor do they keep his commandments. They do not know how to love God and how to put him first in their lives. "God is love; and he that dwelleth in love dwelleth in God, and God in him."[8] Where do you think you would fit in on the list of a person who does not have God listed as number one? Watch out!

Just because someone claims to be a Christian, does not mean that that person is a Christian. Christians bear fruit that prove that they are who they say they are. Beware of those who hang around the church but the church is not in them. Remember, the evil one is seeking whom he may devour.

> Again there was a day when the sons of God came to present themselves before the Lord, and Satan came also among them to present himself before the Lord. And the Lord said unto Satan, From whence comest thou? And Satan answered the Lord, and said, From

---

[8] KJV, I John 4:16

going to and fro in the earth, and from walking up and down in it.[9]

Never marry someone just because they are famous or handsome, or just because it appears that they are well liked by everyone. Everyone might like them and you might like them too, but that does not mean that person is God's best for you. To make an investment of your time and talent into a marriage with the wrong person, who may even be a Christian, would be a loss for you. Your return would be in the negative.

Time is a valuable gift given to us by God. He is holding each of us accountable as stewards over the time he has allotted to us. Be sure to make a godly investment into a godly marriage so that you can receive a godly return.

I have had conversations with Christian men and women who have been devastated to learn that they had married a person, whom they thought to be a Christian, but later found out that the person they married was not the Christian they pretended to be. One person said that

---
[9] KJV, Job 2:1-2

their spouse turned out to be a human devil. It is always sad to see the fall and divorce of the many television religious leaders who have much influence over such large numbers of people around the world. Marriages are always under attack. Divorce in the church is just as common as divorce in the secular world. There was a time when movie stars divorced and remarried on a regular basis, but now this practice has moved into the lives of regular people. All Satan wants is an inch. Now divorce has moved right into the church. Satan was given an inch and that was not enough, so he took a mile. Christians must stop this attack and take authority over this spirit of divorce.

I have had conversations with Christians who are married to Christians who have had ongoing affairs. One person expressed the fact that their spouse tried to keep the extramarital affair hidden for a while but, after more than a year, the affair was flaunted and became more painful than could be expressed. One person's spouse was having an affair with a member in the church where they attended. Another person's spouse was having affairs, more than one, outside of the church. One spouse's affair produced children, more than one. The injured spouse said that the fallen spouse had a history of not spending time at home. There was always some excuse for being away from the immediate family. The excuses ranged from having to go and help others, to being bored at home. When at home with the immediate family, one used the excuse of being too tired and sleepy to spend time in family conversations. This type of behavior is not only painful for the Christian spouse who endures it, but it is also very painful for the children involved. Spouses and children who suffer the betrayal, embarrassment and pain caused by these extramarital affairs often become withdrawn and fearful. They fear what people might say behind their backs. They fear that others will consider them inadequate or less of a person than they really are. The spouse who suffers the injury would not want their friends and family to know that prince charming has failed to be the faithful spouse they were all built up to be. A few of these injured spouses said that they were warned against marrying their spouse before the marriage. These warnings came from family, friends, and clergy. One spouse admitted knowing, after seeking the Lord, that this was not the person to marry. Out of disobedience, the marriage took place and Satan took a seat right in the middle. Many spouses have concluded that lust played a big part in their reason for marriage. Some of them felt things would have turned out differently if they had waited on the Lord. Their impatience got them into a bad fix.

The subject of lust is not a highly discussed topic in the secular world. There are many books and movies that cover sexual topics, but not many are addressing or exposing lust and the devastating affects it has on society. Lust has taken its toll on the world; both the church world and the secular world.

I have spoken with some Christian spouses who have been deeply bruised by infidelity and abuse. One expressed the desire of turning to the same sex for sexual fulfillment, while hoping that the same sex would be more understanding and less likely to inflict the same kind of pain the opposite sex inflicts. Some have committed adultery or incest, and some have lain with animals. These ungodly acts are used to pacify the pains and embarrassment of a failed marriage. These acts are not fulfilling and can never be. The Word of God sets the standard against such acts.

> The man who commits adultery with another's wife, even his neighbor's wife, the adulterer and the adulteress shall surely be put to death. And the man who lies carnally with his father's wife has uncovered his father's nakedness; both of the guilty ones shall surely be put to death; their blood shall be upon their own heads. And if a man lies carnally with his daughter-in-law, both of them shall surely be put to death; they have wrought confusion, perversion, and defilement; their blood shall be upon their own heads. If a man lies with a male as if he were a woman, both men have committed an offense (something perverse, unnatural, abhorrent, and detestable); they shall surely be put to death; their blood shall be upon them. And if a man takes a wife and her mother, it is wickedness and an outrageous offense; all three shall be burned with fire, both he and they [after being stoned to death], that there be no wickedness among you. And if a man lies carnally with a beast, he shall surely be [stoned] to death, and you shall slay the beast. If a woman approaches any beast and lies carnally with it, you shall [stone] the woman and the beast; they shall surely be put to death; their blood is upon them. If a man takes his sister, his father's or his mother's daughter, and sees her nakedness and she sees his nakedness, it is a wicked and shameful thing; and they shall be cut off in the sight of their people; he

has had sexual relations with his sister; he shall bear his iniquity. And if a man shall lie with a woman having her menstrual pains and shall uncover her nakedness, he has made naked her fountain, and she has uncovered the fountain of her blood; and both of them shall be cut off from among their people. You shall not uncover the nakedness of your mother's sister or of your father's sister, for that is to make naked his close kin; they shall bear their iniquity. And if a man shall lie carnally with his uncle's wife, he has uncovered his uncle's nakedness; they shall bear their sin; they shall die childless [not literally, but in a legal sense]. And if a man shall take his brother's wife, it is impurity; he has uncovered his brother's nakedness; they shall be childless [not literally, but in a legal sense]. You shall therefore keep all My statutes and all My ordinances and do them, that the land where I am bringing you to dwell may not vomit you out [as it did those before you]. You shall not walk in the customs of the nation which I am casting out before you; for they did all these things, and therefore I was wearied and grieved by them. But I have said to you, You shall inherit their land, and I will give it to you to possess, a land flowing with milk and honey. I am the Lord your God, Who has separated you from the peoples.[10]

Spouses who commit these sinful acts must pay the consequences. The customs of today's modern society says that everything and anything goes; but God has forbidden his people from following these foul customs.

---

[10] AMP, Leviticus 20:10-24

One Christian spouse told me that the pain and embarrassment was so unbearable that they completely left the church. This spouse acknowledged that very little encouragement came from the church. The church is for the healing of hurting people. Divorced people are in need of rest, peace, family and friends. They do not need more abuse from mouthy, opinionated, religious people. I am in no way granting license to those that want to marry dozens of times just testing the waters in search of someone to enslave. There are people that have hit hard times in their marriage, faced divorce, no fault of their own, and have been treated as outcasts by the church. If Christians turn them away, there are other doors opened to receive them. Let us open the door of love. Love will heal and bring about a change for the good.

One of the Christian spouses sought healing that was other than spiritual. This person was just as angry as they were hurt. They operated through strife and did many spiteful things while trying to get even. They felt they could never forget how badly bruised they were by statements made by church folk. They explained that only one side of the story was told and no one seemed to show pity or even a desire to help them be restored as a couple. Many times well meaning Christians can do more damage than can be imagined. Before statements are made concerning such personal and sensitive situations, it is important to pray specifically for the parties involved and specifically concerning the situation. Different religious groups have different rules concerning divorce; however, the Word of God remains the same.

There are times when divorce occurs. There are times when the non-Christian spouse applies for the divorce, and there are times when the Christian spouse applies for the divorce. Some of the conversations mentioned in this book, concerning the abuse received by some of the spouses, were very painful for me to hear and for me to write. This book is not suggesting that anyone should accept abuse or even stay in an abusive situation. It is written to tell Christians how to survive a marriage with a non-Christian spouse. It gives examples of Christians who survived and what it took for them to survive.

There are times when the Christian walks in disobedience by marrying a non-Christian. There are many different scenarios, many different excuses, many ifs, ands, and buts; but the Word of God remains the same. We are to apply God's Word to our own lives and not judge others by our own self-righteousness.

> THEREFORE YOU have no excuse or defense or justification, O man, whoever you are who judges and condemns another. For in posing as judge and passing sentence on another, you condemn yourself, because you who judge are habitually practicing the very same things [that you censure and denounce].[11]

To look down on another's shortcoming or downfall in a manner of scorn, and to say, "I would never do that," or "I would never divorce," or "that could never happen to me," is judging. To say these kinds of things would imply that the person who encounters such hardness deserves it, or that you are better than they are. I am sure that most people do not enter into a marriage with the intentions of being abused, betrayed or divorced, but these things do happen; sometimes we are at fault and sometimes we are not. Regardless of who is at fault, the best place to go is to God. Many people have turned to

---

[11] AMP, Romans 2:1

him and have received more help than they dreamed to be possible.

CHAPTER III

HOW TO SURVIVE

Finally, my brethren, be strong in the Lord, and in the power of his might. Put on the whole armor of God, that ye may be able to stand against the wiles of the devil.[1]

Wherefore take unto you the whole armor of God, that ye may be able to withstand in the evil day, and having done all, to stand. Stand therefore, having your loins girt about with truth, and having on the breastplate of righteousness; And your feet shod with the preparation of the gospel of peace; Above all, taking the shield of faith, wherewith ye shall be able to quench all the fiery darts of the wicked. And take the helmet of salvation, and the sword of the Spirit, which is the word of God: Praying always with all prayer and supplication in the Spirit, and watching thereunto with all perseverance and supplication for all saints; And for me, that utterance may be given unto me, that I

---

[1] KJV, Ephesians 6:10-11

may open my mouth boldly, to make known the mystery of the gospel, For which I am an ambassador in bonds: that therein I may speak boldly, as I ought to speak.[2]

The Apostle Paul wrote a letter to the saints who were at Ephesus, the capital of the chief province of Asia, admonishing them to be armed in order to stand in the evil day. Just as Paul admonished the saints at Ephesus to be armed, the same admonition goes for the Christians of today.

Many marriages have faced evil days and fiery darts. It is most wonderful to see both husband and wife fighting the evils that come to attack their marriage. When both husband and wife are fully armed with the whole armor of God, which is Jesus Christ, they share in the fight and are able to encourage one another. When the marriage between the Christian and the non-Christian comes under an attack from the wicked, it is the Christian spouse who faces the brunt of the battle and has to endure the many attacks, and most of the time alone. It is most important that Christians seek God's guidance when selecting prayer warriors or even a prayer partner to join

---

[2] KJV, Ephesians 6:13-20

in for spiritual support. The Lord would have the Christian spouse to be encouraged in the battle and to have a victorious outcome. Choosing a prayer partner or prayer warriors on your own could possibly be more detrimental than fighting alone. There are those who mean well but do not have the wisdom of God concerning your situation.

Christian marriages have something in common that the Christian and non-Christian marriages do not. The Christian marriages have salvation; whereas, the Christian and the non-Christian marriages are spiritually mismatched, one spouse has salvation and the other spouse does not. A Christian who is in a spiritually mismatched marriage, whether intentionally or unintentionally, can survive.

In order to survive the wicked attacks and to stand in the evil day, we must love God and put him first. Proverbs 3:6-7 tells us to trust in the Lord with all of our heart and not lean on our own understanding; to acknowledge him in all of our ways and he shall direct our path. If we trust him and put him first, he will be with us and lead us through the dark and evil day. It is the enemy's job to provide a forge for war against the marriage. Satan loves to cause a heated battle in the midst of marriages. There are examples in the scriptures that give wisdom concerning the things couples can do to prevent big blow-ups during times of disagreement. "A soft answer turneth away wrath: but grievous words stir up anger. The tongue of the wise useth knowledge aright: but the mouth of fools poureth out foolishness."[3] "A wholesome tongue is a tree of life: but perverseness therein is a breach in the spirit."[4]

> For in many things we offend all. If any man offend not in word, the same is a perfect man, and able also to bridle the whole body. Behold, we put bits in the horses' mouths, that they may obey us; and we turn about their whole body. Behold also the ships, which though they be so great, and are driven of fierce winds, yet are they turned about with a very small helm, whithersoever the governor listeth. Even so the tongue is a little member, and boasteth great things. Behold, how great a matter a little fire kindleth! And the tongue is a fire, a world of iniquity; so is the tongue among our members, that it defileth the whole body, and setteth on fire the course of nature; and it is set on fire of hell. For every kind of beasts,

---

[3] KJV, Proverbs 15:1-2
[4] KJV, Proverbs 15:4

and of birds, and of serpents, and of things in the sea, is tamed, and hath been tamed of mankind: But the tongue can no man tame; it is an unruly evil, full of deadly poison. Therewith bless we God, even the Father; and therewith curse we men, which are made after the similitude of God. Out of the same mouth proceedeth blessing and cursing. My brethren, these things ought not so to be. Doth a fountain send forth at the same place sweet water and bitter? Can a fig tree, my brethren, bear olive berries? either a vine, figs? So can no fountain both yield salt water and fresh. Who is a wise man and endued with knowledge among you? let him show out of a good conversation his works with meekness of wisdom.[5]

The tongue plays a vital role in marriage relationships. One word can set the atmosphere for romance or it can kill any hope there might have been for a spark of romance. One word can bring peace into the marriage or it can cause the marriage to be dissolved. In the scriptures, James tells us that the whole body of a large horse is controlled by the bit we put in the horses' mouth. If mankind would get the principle thing, which is wisdom, and control the tongue, then mankind would miss out on a lot of grief and pain. Where there is no control over the tongue, there is no control over the body. This is a very powerful statement. If a person has no control over

---
[5] KJV, James 3:2-13

the things that come out of their mouth, they have no control over their body. They misuse their body and they use their body in any way they see fit because they have no control over their tongue. James goes on to tell us that mankind has been able to tame every kind of beast, birds, serpents, and things in the sea, but cannot tame his own tongue. James says that the tongue is an unruly evil and that it is full of deadly poison. The evil that attacks marriages is sometimes the tongue and not always the devil. Let us not lie on the devil. He is a liar all by himself. We often invite trouble into our marriages by way of the tongue. Let us practice taking control over our tongue and allowing the Lord to give us the words to say.

One of the Christian spouses told me of the verbal abuse that had gone on for a long period of time and how the wisdom of God put an end to the abuse. The lack of communications, miscommunications, or even the inability to communicate in a marriage has caused disagreements, harsh arguments, physical fights and, in some instances, divorce. One non-Christian spouse told me that the attitude and smart-mouth answers given by the

How To Survive A Marriage
With A Non-Christian Spouse

Christian spouse caused the non-Christian spouse to physically knock the Christian spouse into near unconsciousness. Regardless of the attitudes or smart-mouth answers, there is never a good enough reason to physically confront one another. No one should ever have to accept a physical attack as punishment for having an attitude or for giving a sassy answer. This is not to excuse spouses, whether Christian or non-Christian, for the display of bad attitudes or smart-mouth answers, but to set the record straight. When the spouse was a child, a spanking might have taken place; but as adults we must always remember, the last spanking took place during childhood. One Christian spouse had numerous bouts with physical attacks after being married for only three months. At first, it was felt that these attacks would eventually end, so no action was taken. These attacks became more frequent and more violent. Family and friends had no idea of what was going on. It is very common for an abused spouse to keep these abuses confidential. There are many reasons for such secrecy. In some cases, the abused spouse would rather suffer the abuse than for anyone to find out exactly what kind of person they have married. In this case, the Christian spouse was warned about the abusive background displayed by one of the parents and some of the siblings, but the Christian spouse disregarded the warning. Rather than being embarrassed and having to hear the words, "I told you so," the Christian spouse decided to roll with the punches. This is so sad, but also unnecessary. The Christian spouse never fought back physically, but one day got tired of the abuse and decided to have other Christians give support in prayer. The way this spouse survived was by the wisdom of God and God's mercy and grace. God's grace is sufficient for all.

> Three times I called upon the Lord and besought [Him] about this and begged that it might depart from me. But He said to me, My grace – My favor and loving-kindness and mercy – are enough for you, [that is, sufficient against any danger and to enable you to bear the trouble manfully]; for My strength and power are made perfect – fulfilled and completed and show themselves most effective – in [your] weakness. Therefore, I will all the more gladly glory in my weaknesses and infirmities, that the strength and power of Christ, the Messiah, may rest – yes, may pitch a tent [over] and dwell – upon me! So for the sake of Christ, I am well pleased and take pleasure in infirmities, insults, hardships, persecutions, perplexities and distresses; for when I am weak (in

human strength), then am I [truly] strong – able, powerful in divine strength.[6]

This Christian spouse spent many days fasting, praying, repenting and searching the scriptures for comfort and reassurance that God's grace and mercy were still available, even after being disobedient. This Christian spouse learned the hard way that there is a price to pay when you enter into a mismatched marriage. Family members found out and became involved. The law enforcement officers became involved. Most of all, God was involved because he was invited and acknowledged as being more than able to deliver. The saints of God bombarded the enemy's artillery of weapons and put him out of business in that Christian's home. One morning the non-Christian spouse woke up from a deep sleep and something had taken place; a change of heart and a change of mind. The non-Christian spouse accepted the Lord Jesus as savior and is now a Christian. No more physical confrontations. The only fight that goes on now, is the good fight of faith.

---

[6] AMP, II Corinthians 12:8-10

Let us take a look at what happened to the Christian husband and wife who were members of the same church, as mentioned in chapter two of this book, one of whom left the household of faith because they felt that they could not take the unfaithfulness of the spouse with another member of the church any longer. I must say that whenever someone leaves God because of the way a person treats them, this is what I call "charging God foolishly." It is not God's fault, will, nor is it God's desire for us to be treated any way other than being esteemed as dear children of God. The unfaithful Christian spouse tried to use discretion while having numerous affairs with a member of the church as well as persons outside of the church; as if being unfaithful is okay as long as you are discrete about it. I must remind you, that I am purposely writing most of this book as being gender neutral. The pendulum in some of these cases has swung freely, to and fro. The pendulum of strife and spite swung quit freely in this particular case. The use of a pendulum to regulate clock movement is in order and serves the intended purpose, but to try and prove the point "anything you can do, I can do better," defeats the purpose. Never will such actions solve the problem. The betrayed spouse purposed in their heart to show how it feels to be hurt beyond measure and hoped that after such pain was inflicted on the betrayer, that the betrayer would change their ways and become faithful. After the pendulum swung a few times, things got worse. The unfaithfulness increased and seven more spirits worse than the one named "unfaithful" entered into that marriage. Other children were born outside of the marriage, which leaves a scar that only God, by His Spirit, can heal. Drugs, separation, mental illness and rage entered. These spirits walked in, took a seat and made full manifestation in the lives of this dear couple. Sickness, poverty, accidents and death were allowed to enter through the door that was left opened. The enemy knocked on the door and presented forbidden fruit, just like he did to Eve in the Garden of Eden. The wedding vows and the Word of God forbid unfaithfulness. The spouse who first started having the affairs, of course, made all kinds of excuses as to why the affairs occurred; and as you would probably guess, the excuse was that it was their spouse's fault. All of the blame was placed on their spouse. They said that their spouse was sickly, unaffectionate and never had time for them, so they felt it to be okay to step outside of the marriage to get the attention and affection they needed. It is true that spouses must spend time together and meet the needs of each other in order to keep the evil one out of the marriage. Hurting people can be selfish people. They focus on their own feelings, their pain and embarrassment, but often fail to see the anguish in others due to their selfish actions. When you hurt, those who are concerned about you hurt also. In this case, the children involved were emotionally damaged. The outrageous behavior of this couple was appalling to all who came in contact with them. One of them finally came to their wits end and discovered that the things they had done were not worth it after all. This one spouse returned to the faith and repented of charging God foolishly concerning the betrayal they had faced. This particular spouse said that they began to think about Jesus' betrayal by Judas, and thought within themselves that Jesus must have really loved the world in order to have allowed himself to suffer such a betrayal. Betrayal is one of the worst inner hurts mankind can experience. There is a twist to this case. This marriage ended in separation, probably not what you had hoped for or expected to read in this book. Everyone expects to read a fairytale ending when they read religious material. Remember, the title of this book is "How To Survive a Marriage with a Non-Christian Spouse." The title of this book is the twist. I am inserting this information for you at this time because it is important for you to remember the aim of this book is to tell you how to survive the marriage, with the emphasis being placed on you and not the marriage.

I have studied cases where people have lost their mind and their life because of the stress and pressure of being married to a non-Christian spouse. Some of them worked so hard at trying to save their marriage until they were not able to survive; needless to say, when a person's focus is on their circumstances and not on the Lord who is able to fix all things, they are in store for a rude awakening. They often suffer the loss of their health, their senses, and eventually end up unfit for the marriage they are trying to save or even for any future marriage. This type of loss is unnecessary when the Lord is our hope. You do not have to lose your mind, die or kill someone when your marriage gets in trouble. You can survive even if the marriage does not.

Christian spouses have the upper hand, which seats the Christian in the position of advantage over the non-Christian spouse. The upper-hand advantage comes from a right-standing relationship with Father God. The Christian spouse has the ear and heart of God at all times, if only they would store this in their memory bank. This fellowship and communion we have with the Father allows us the opportunity to receive instructions from Him. Christian spouses can survive by following the directions given to them in the written Word of God. The following scripture is giving sound counsel to married couples.

> IN LIKE manner, you married women, be submissive to your own husbands [subordinate yourselves as being secondary to and dependent on them, and adapt yourselves to them], so that even if any do not obey the Word [of God], they may be won over not by discussion but by the [godly] lives of their wives. When they observe the pure and modest way in which you conduct yourselves, together with your reverence [for your husband; you are to feel for him all that reverence includes: to respect, defer to, revere him – to

honor, esteem, appreciate, prize, and, in the human sense, to adore him, that is, to admire, praise, be devoted to, deeply love, and enjoy your husband]. It was thus that Sarah obeyed Abraham [following his guidance and acknowledging his headship over her by] calling him lord (master, leader, authority). And you are now her true daughters if you do right and let nothing terrify you [not giving way to hysterical fears or letting anxieties unnerve you]. In the same way you married men should live considerately with [your wives], with an intelligent recognition [of the marriage relation], honoring the woman as [physically] the weaker, but [realizing that you] are joint heirs of the grace of (God's unmerited favor) of life, in order that your prayers may not be hindered and cut off. [Otherwise you cannot pray effectively.] Finally, all [of you] should be of one and the same mind [united in spirit], sympathizing [with one another], loving [each other] as brethren [of one household], compassionate and courteous (tenderhearted and humble). Never return evil for evil or insult for insult (scolding, tongue-lashing, berating), but on the contrary blessing [praying for their welfare, happiness, and protection, and truly pitying and loving them]. For know that to this you have been called, that you may yourselves inherit a blessing [from God – that you may obtain a blessing as heirs, bringing welfare and happiness and protection]. For let him who wants to enjoy life and see good days [good – whether apparent or not] keep his tongue free from evil and his lips from guile (treachery, deceit).[7]

---

[7] AMP, I Peter 3:1-2, 6-10

If the above scripture were to be adhered to by both spouses, there most certainly would be enough harmony, love and peace to last a lifetime. To make things work out God's way, we must adhere to God's ways. Each spouse is responsible for doing what the Word of God has instructed them to do.

Many couples enter into the marriage with preconceived ideas; in other words, they have their own ideas of how things are going to be run in their household. It appears that some spouses fail to remember that they are married to a person who has a personality, a brain, and some ideas of their own. Each person has their own way of expressing their feelings and releasing the pressures they face from day to day.

One of the couples mentioned in the previous chapter had a more serious problem concerning the differences in the way men and women think. One of the spouses claimed to have cared less about the thoughts and opinions of the other spouse. This was a bad mistake. Another party entered the picture and was very much concerned and interested in the thoughts and opinions of that person's spouse. Much prayer, fasting and warfare went forth in an effort to recover the loss. The spouse who was so carefree had to repent and correct their way of thinking. In this case, that spouse had to put forth extra efforts in every area of their marriage in order to repair the damage that had been done. This spouse did overcome the damage that was done and is still being diligent in learning to participate in the activities that their spouse has interest.

To survive, a person must put forth an effort. Survivors never allow situations to get the upper hand. Survivors plan and strategize the demise of the foe. They set their minds to achieve the trophy. They see themselves winning. Many of the spouses, with whom I spoke, had to really read and study the Word of God, pray and fast, and get help from other trustworthy Christians. This is how they were able to continue to stand and keep their sanity. A few of them said that they were very discouraged and felt like giving up, but after receiving spiritual help, they were strengthened for the journey. They continued on their journey and survived. Mind you, they survived. A couple of the marriages did not survive, but the spouses who put their trust in the True and Living God survived and are doing very well. One of the Christian spouses being discussed in this book has survived and has gone on to be famous in the religious field, even though the marriage did not survive. This spouse learned to trust in the Lord and to do good deeds toward their spouse and not to do evil. This spouse learned that it does not pay to take the eye – for-an-eye approach.

> For we know Him Who said, Vengeance is Mine [retribution and the meting out of full justice rest with Me]; I will exact the compensation], says the Lord. And again, The Lord will judge and determine and solve and settle the cause and the cases of His people. [Deut. 32:35, 36.] It is a fearful (formidable and terrible) thing to incur the divine penalties and be cast into the hands of the living God! But be ever mindful of the days gone by in which, after you were first spiritually enlightened, you endured a great and painful struggle, Sometimes being yourselves a gazingstock, publicly exposed to insults and abuse and distress, and sometimes claiming fellowship and making common cause with others who were so treated. For you did sympathize and suffer along with those who were imprisoned, and you bore cheerfully the plundering of your belongings and the confiscation of your property, in the

knowledge and consciousness that you yourselves had a better and lasting possession. Do not, therefore, fling away your fearless confidence, for it carries a great and glorious compensation of reward. For you have need of steadfast patience and endurance, so that you may perform and fully accomplish the will of God, and thus receive and carry away [and enjoy to the full] what is promised. For still a little while (a very little while), and the Coming One will come and He will not delay. But the just shall live by faith [My righteous servant shall live by his conviction respecting man's relationship to God and divine things, and holy fervor born of faith and conjoined with it]: and if he draws back and shrinks in fear, My soul has no delight or pleasure in him. [Hab. 2:3-4.] But our way is not that of those who draw back to eternal misery (perdition) and are utterly destroyed, but we are of those who believe [who cleave to and trust in and rely on God through Jesus Christ, the Messiah] and by faith preserve the soul.[8]

The surviving spouses agreed that, although painful, the process of going through their marital problems stripped away pride and other things that kept them out of the place God had for them. They discovered the prize of being in that holy place, that secret place, that place of peace with God, when they humbled themselves

---

[8] AMP, Hebrews 10:30-39

to seek after God and his righteousness. They had come to their wits end, but discovered that the entrance of God's word gave them understanding and discernment. They were empowered supernaturally to better comprehend the will of God concerning their lives. The revelation of God's word, which is His will, gave them great peace because they trusted in God and knew that God would work all things for their good.

Some surviving spouses learned that having the last word is not so important after all. The truth will always surface, maybe not when a person thinks it should, but it eventually surfaces to save the day. It takes more grace and intelligence to allow another person to have the last say than it does to open one's mouth and insert a foot. Once this lesson was learned, the spouses realized the strength they had obtained by letting their spouse have the last say. This is strength, not weakness.

In order to survive, one survivor explained that their faith and confidence was in God and God alone. It was not always this way. There were times, they explained, their faith, hope and trust was in their spouse, not in God. This person learned that God's word and promises must always be fresh in our heart. A spirit of prayer and thanksgiving should always be offered unto the Lord as a sacrifice, even when we are at the lowest point of our lives. This is what this spouse did, and this is how they survived. God continues to bring forth deliverance to the spouses, and to the children born into these marriages. Thank God for the spirit of God that enables us to survive. May His spirit spread across the land and cause the people to survive.

CHAPTER IV

TO THE SINGLES

This chapter is prayerfully dedicated to those who are single, although it should be of interest to everyone. Even the married person started off being single. Being single is a very precious and important time in life. When some single people think of being single, they think of being lonely and undesirable. They seldom think about the good plan that God has for their life and that the preparation for God's plan is in the making. The devil is a liar. He tells the singles that they must marry as soon as possible; forget counseling and all other necessary steps that would help prevent a shipwreck of a marriage. He wants the singles to believe that they are going to die young, even before they have a chance to marry and have children. His plan is to cause mankind to deviate from the perfect will of God.

Satan works in deceit. He wants to convince the singles that they are less than desirable. This trick causes the singles to have low self-esteem. After low self-esteem sets in, sexual sins usually follow. Singles can often become so desperate, that they accept the lowest of characters in their lives. Some feel that being single is a disgrace. This is not true.

> And in that day seven women shall take hold of one man, saying, We will eat our own bread and provide our own apparel; only let us be called by your name to take away our reproach [of being unmarried].[1]

This scripture was written many hundreds of years ago. There is nothing new under the sun, and that includes marriages and singleness.

---

[1] AMP, Isaiah 4:1

How To Survive A Marriage
With A Non-Christian Spouse

Let me encourage you singles, you are God's creation. You are wonderfully and wondrously made according to God's divine blueprint. If there is an undesirable one, it is Satan, not you.

Singles, please read and study the previous chapters well before entering into a relationship that could possibly lead to marriage. Remember the warning signs that some of the married couples seemed to have missed. Learn from the pitfalls of others without condemning and belittling them. The couples mentioned in this book paid a price for their actions. Know that everyone has to give an account for every deed they do and every word they speak. Taking heed to the experiences given in this book can help you avoid paying the high price of pain and shame.

Here is some advice that will take you a long way in life:

Dedicate your life, spirit, body and soul to the Lord. You have been bought with the blood of Jesus, therefore, that makes you very valuable. Ask the Father for a spouse who has done the same.

Pray always to the Father, in the name of Jesus Christ. He is your personal savior. He is able to keep you from falling and to present you blameless before the Father. Ask the Father for a spouse who is of the same mind to be kept by the Lord.

Be faithful to the Lord and keep His commandments; this is loving Him. Ask the Father for a spouse who is obedient to the Lord and who loves Him. In every situation, give thanks to the Lord; learning to avoid murmuring and complaining. Ask for a spouse who does the same.

Trust in the Lord and set your affections upon Him. He will add to you the things you need and the things the gentiles seek after. Ask the Father for a spouse who walks in this area of faith.

If you desire a spouse, seek the Lord first. Go through the proper protocol and do not forsake premarital counseling. Ask for a spouse who is willing to do the same.

How To Survive A Marriage
With A Non-Christian Spouse

Do not plan on eloping. When singles get the feeling that someone is in disagreement with the person they choose, there is a tendency to withdraw into secrecy. This type of behavior breeds trouble. Remember what happened in an earlier chapter? After marriage, abuse starts and the secrecy continues. This secrecy is due to embarrassment and is an attempt to avoid being reminded of how the mistake came into being.

Demand and give respect. Ask the Father for a spouse who is proficient in this area. Be patient and wait on the Lord; He will strengthen you as you wait. Ask the Father for a spouse who is mature in this area.

When the Lord gives you the green light, go for it without delay. Ask for a spouse who has godly wisdom and is able to discern and act upon the Word of the Lord. It is very important that couples be able to discern the time that God has ordained for them to receive the promise.

Most of all, after you are blessed, remember the Lord. Ask the Father for a spouse who will keep the Lord before them at all times.

If your desire is to please the Lord and remain single, this desire is not a sin. May God bless and keep you. God will keep you as you continue to commit your ways unto Him. Singles, are you willing to abide by the vows that are required of you at the time of the marriage? Are you willing to share yourself and your possessions with your spouse and children, if there be any? Are you willing to give the time that is required when you have a family? Are you prepared and willing to accept the responsibility of a family? Are you willing to work at being married? Being married is one of the most wonderful unions there could possibly be. Marriages must be worked on in order for them to last. Are you a fighter or one who throws in the towel when things do not go your way? If yes, you are the one who throws in the towel, then you had better pray some more and wait a while longer before you consider marriage. Most people who want to get married will pray for the kind of spouse they would like to marry, and this is the proper thing to do. I wonder, though, how many of them pray for the Lord to prepare them to be the kind of spouse the Lord would have them to be. We pray and ask the Lord to bless us with a wonderful spouse. This is a good thing to pray for. We should also pray and ask the Lord to make us a wonderful spouse for the person we marry. This type of prayer is an unselfish prayer, a sign of being considerate and mature.

I believe those who read this book will benefit from the experiences of others. My desire is that the singles who read it gain knowledge concerning the seriousness of marriage and relationship. My prayer for the singles is that they seek to please God and not man; that they seek God's will, plan, and purpose, and not that of man; that God will keep them, bless them, and show Himself mightily through them; that, if they desire to remain single, negative words and condemning words that come their way, because of their singleness, be of non-effect. I pray that the fear of marriage be cast out in the mighty name of Jesus Christ, and that all of the negative rumors and horror stories they have heard or the things they have witnessed concerning failed marriages are ineffective in their lives. I pray love and peace over them, right now. In Jesus Name. Amen.

How To Survive A Marriage
With A Non-Christian Spouse

CHAPTER V

CONCLUSION

REMEMBER [earnestly] also your Creator [that you are not your own, but His property now] in the days of your youth, before the evil days come or the years draw near when you will say [of physical pleasures], I have no enjoyment in them-[II Sam. 19:35.] Before the sun and the light and the moon and the stars are darkened [sight is impaired], and the clouds [of depression] return after the rain [of tears]; In the day when the keepers of the house [the hands and the arms] tremble, and the strong men [the feet and the knees] bow themselves, and the grinders [the molar teeth] cease because they are few, and those who look out of the windows [the eyes] are darkened; When the doors [the lips] are shut in the streets and the sound of the grinding [of the teeth] is low, and one rises up at the voice of a bird and the crowing of a cock, and all the daughters of music [the voice and the ear] are brought low; Also when [the old] are afraid of danger from that which is high, and fears are in the way, and the almond tree [their white hair] blooms, and the grasshopper [a little thing] is a burden, and desire and appetite fail, because man goes to his everlasting home and the mourners go about the streets or marketplaces. [Job 17:13.] [Remember your Creator earnestly now] before the silver cord [of life] is snapped apart, or the golden bowl is broken, or the pitcher is broken at the fountain, or the wheel broken at the cistern [and the whole circulatory system of the blood ceases to function]; Then shall the dust [out of which God made man's body] return to the earth as it was, and the spirit shall return to God Who gave it.[1]

King Solomon gives words of wisdom to all who will take heed. After all is said and done, it behooves us to conclude the whole matter with the same conclusion reached by King Solomon, "Fear God, and keep his commandments: for this is the whole duty of man. For God shall bring every work into judgment, with every secret thing, whether it be good, or whether it be evil."[2]

The Amplified version says:

> All has been heard; the end of the matter is: Fear God [revere and worship Him, knowing that He is] and keep His commandments, for this is the whole of man [the full, original purpose of his creation, the object of God's

---

[1] AMP, Ecclesiastes 12:1-7
[2] KJV, Ecclesiastes 12:13

providence, the root of character, the foundation of all happiness, the adjustment to all inharmonious circumstances and conditions under the sun] and the whole [duty] for every man. For God shall bring every work into judgment, with every secret thing, whether it is good or evil.[3]

King Solomon is warning us about the dangers of not restraining our fleshly desires. Solomon knew about the dangers of giving in to those sinful, fleshly desires because of his own personal experiences.

> But king Solomon loved many strange women, together with the daughter of Pharaoh, women of the Moabites, Ammonites, Edomites, Zidonians, and Hittites; Of the nations concerning which the Lord said unto the children of Israel, Ye shall not go in to them, neither shall they come in unto you: for surely they will turn away your heart after their gods: Solomon cleaved unto these in love. And he had seven hundred wives, princesses, and three hundred concubines: and his wives turned away his heart. For it came to pass, when Solomon was old, that his wives turned away his heart after other gods: and his heart was not perfect with the Lord his God, as was the heart of David his father. For Solomon went after Ashtoreth the goddess of the Zidonians, and after Milcom the abomination of the Ammonites. And Solomon did evil in the

---

[3] AMP, Ecclesiastes 12:13-14

sight of the Lord, and went not fully after the Lord, as did David his father. Then did Solomon build a high place for Chemosh, the abomination of Moab, in the hill that is before Jerusalem, and for Molech, the abomination of the Children of Ammon. And likewise did he for all his strange wives, which burnt incense and sacrificed unto their gods. And the Lord was angry with Solomon, because his heart was turned from the Lord God of Israel, which had appeared unto him twice, And had commanded him concerning this thing, that he should not go after other gods: but he kept not that which the Lord commanded. Wherefore the Lord said unto Solomon, Forasmuch as this is done of thee and thou hast not kept my covenant and my statutes, which I have commanded thee, I will surely rend the kingdom from thee, and will give it to thy servant.[4]

Although Solomon sends this warning out to young men and young women, there are many old men and old women who need to receive this warning as well. I have not reached the age of experiencing this saying, but I have heard the saying, "Just because there is snow on the roof does not mean there is no fire in the furnace." Satan will pull every trick available just to cause a soul to sin. He could care less about the age. It is most sad to see the elderly, the ones who should be giving sound advice to the youth, trying to be sensually sexy, or trying to seduce our youth, or committing lewd acts without shame.

---

[4] KJV, I Kings 11:1-11

How To Survive A Marriage
With A Non-Christian Spouse

King Solomon is not only concluding the whole matter as he warns us to remember our creator, he is also nearing the end of his days and can see his past clearly. Remember, hindsight vision is 20/20. After making a mistake, it is often easy to pinpoint the reason the mistake occurred or what could have prevented the mistake from occurring. Well, here is the chance to prevent a real shipwreck in present and future relationships. Fearing God reverently and keeping his commandments will pay off in the present and also in the future. Living a godly life in the present will cause the blessings of God to be upon you now and in the future. Living a godly life in the present will enable you to look back with joy and not with regret and sorrow. Solomon tells us that God shall bring every work into judgment, with every secret thing, whether it be good, or evil. Everyone would be glad to know that only their good work would be brought into judgment and every evil thing would never be brought forward; therefore, everyone would get their great reward and not be judged for their evil. It does not work that way.

> Evil shall slay the wicked: and they that hate the righteous shall be desolate. The Lord redeemeth the soul of his servants: and none of them that trust in him shall be desolate.[5]

Those who practice evil and fail to repent of the evil shall be destroyed by evil. God's will for his people is that they overcome evil. Even in the marriage, God's will is that his people would overcome the evil. For those whose marriages ended in divorce, God's will is that his servants overcome the evil, survive, and depend upon him. The Lord continuously rescues the soul of his servants. The soul consists of the will, the mind, and the emotions. God continuously delivers the will, mind, and emotions of his servants from the evil that seeks to destroy the seed of God that has been planted in his servants. Guard your soul from ungodly communications, whether it be from the television or radio, reading materials, conversations that you would not want Jesus to hear, or evil imaginations; these things will cause your demise. The whole purpose is to survive God's way.

Here are a few points to keep in mind as you strive to survive a marriage with a non-Christian spouse:

---

[5] KJV, Psalm 34:21-22

How To Survive A Marriage
With A Non-Christian Spouse

Keep your heart pure regardless of what comes your way. You will have to swallow your pride and remember that Jesus bore your shame many, many years ago when His clothes were stripped from His body, He was scourged, spit on, laughed at and mocked for you. He went through this horror just for you. Yes, it is personal. Swallowing your pride does not mean that you are a weak person, it shows your strength. If you are a Christian and your goal is to see Jesus in peace, then you really want your heart to be pure. Ask the Lord for help. You have his ear. He will hear and he will help. Humble yourself and ask him.

Think before you act upon or react to the behavior of your non-Christian spouse. Reacting or speaking out of your emotions before you take the time to think can prove to be destructive to your relationship. Many have spoken words that they really did not mean to say and were sorry later. Many have reacted physically and were sorry later. In some cases, later was too late.

Examine your motives. When you speak or react to a situation with your spouse, be sure to examine the response you gave and the behavior you portrayed. Be sure you are able to identify who was in charge of your being as you spoke or reacted. Was it your flesh or did you allow the leading of the Holy Spirit? Allowing the leading of the Holy Spirit does not mean you allowed your spouse to abuse you. God gives wisdom to those who ask for it and he will not rebuke them for asking.

Repent of your sins. Submit to God and resist the devil and the devil will flee. Most of the time, when couples are faced with marital distress, they say and do things that are not pleasing to the Lord. In other words, they need to confess their faults and repent to the Lord and to their spouse for their behavior. Holding on to anger and bitterness causes sickness in the body, the mind, the family unit, and in the church. We must rid ourselves of all the things that cause sickness.

Obtain Christian counseling. It is hard to think clearly when you are in the midst of a marital dilemma. Right seems wrong, and wrong seems right. Panic sets in and the sense of direction becomes obscured. It is easy to make a wrong decision when you are hurt or angry. It seems easier to just walk away from the situation and just give up the kids, the cars, the house, the money, the clothes, the job, and even the Jesus who really loves you and who brought you through many storms before this one hit the horizon. It seems easier to just give up and quit; but this is really the hard way. This is the way that will haunt you for the rest of your life. It might seem easier to just kill yourself and everybody who is involved; but this would never end things for you. Remember your wedding vows? The minister stated, "I require and charge you both, as ye will answer at the dreadful day of judgment, when the secrets of all hearts shall be disclosed...." Remember that portion, or did a fit of anger, hurt, or an emotional glitch take over your senses, or did you forget? You are held accountable to God for the care and responsibility you owe to your family. You need good Christian counseling to help you see things God's way. The Christian counselor will walk you through God's Word and help pray you through the process of deliverance. The steps in the process of counseling will allow you to face the real truth; the kind of truth that might not make you feel good right away, but it will surely make you free if you will accept it.

Synchronize your walk and your way of thinking with the Word of God. You are more than a conqueror through Jesus Christ. You are victorious and complete in him. There is no scripture that justifies your defeat. Do not lose this battle by default. You default if you give up and quit. Be stubborn enough to stick with the Lord. Never give up on your Lord and Savior. He is with you always, in the fire and out of the fire.

Never let others put a guilt trip on you by telling you that the Joneses handled their marital problems differently and they got better results than you. People often mean well, but they can be so rude and misinformed. Please forgive them. You must remember that you and your spouse just happened not to be the Joneses and your situation is unique to you and your spouse. Just stay saved and stay close to the Lord. Never allow people to judge your salvation according to the testing of your marriage. Some people have been crushed by statements made to them by well meaning, uninformed Christians. Some Christians feel that the Christian spouse has sin in their life or they must be an awful person if their spouse happens to be a non-Christian. You do not have to divorce nor mistreat your spouse because they are a non-Christian; do not allow silly nonsense to cause unnecessary conflict between you and your spouse. There are couples, one Christian and the other non-Christian, who get along without arguing and fighting. Keep praying and allow the light of God in you to draw your spouse. May I encourage you to look to the Lord. He is your sufficiency. He is willing and more than able to save the lost.

Many spouses have been saved and many marriages have been healed, and we give God the praise, honor, and glory.

My desire is that each of us keep in mind that there are those Christian spouses who are trusting, hoping, and praying for the deliverance of their spouses; some of them for many, many years. Let us keep them girded with prayer and the Word of God. Let us allow the Holy Spirit to season the words we speak to them with grace and wisdom.

I pray that each of you have been informed, blessed and encouraged by the material included in this book. Whether you are male or female, married, single, or divorced, may I again stress that the main topic of this book is how to survive a marriage with a non-Christian spouse; with special emphasis placed on the word "survive." I would like to place a very special emphasis on a word in the title of this book that you may not readily see. That word, as a matter of fact, is most important. It is hidden. It is invisible. It is implied. That word is "you." You can survive. You can be a whole person in Christ Jesus, and you can be victorious.

If you want to see the move of God in your life as never before, start applying the Word of God to every area of your life; do not wait for tomorrow, start today.

Your confession should be:

"In Him I am complete."

"His thoughts toward me are good and not evil."

"God has a good plan for my life."

Your testimony should be: "The Word of God encourages me to stand, to take courage, to be strong in times of trouble; therefore, I stand."

We are to pray and not faint. Instead of being fretful, we are to be thankful and rejoice in the God of our salvation.

Because of the power that is in the blood of Jesus, and in the name of Jesus, and in the Word of God, and in the words of our testimony, and because Jesus defeated Satan for us, we can boldly say, "I am a survivor." When this life is over, we want to be able to rejoice in the Lord and say, "Thank you Jesus!" "Glory to God!" "I survived!"

NOTES AND COMMENTS

Before you get involved in a relationship, you should consider providing input to the following items. This section is provided for you to add your comments and notes concerning these items.

People have feelings and feelings are not to be played upon nor taken for granted.

QUESTION: Have you ever been the victim? _____

_____

_____

_____

_____

_____

If your answer is yes, how did you feel? _____   ___

_____

_____

_____

_____

_____

Did you forgive or did you hurt others so they could feel the pain you felt? _____

_____

_____

_____

_____

_____

You might not be serious about the relationship, but the other person might be very serious and under the impression that you are just as serious. Say what you mean and do not beat around the bush in hopes that the other person can read between the lines.

COMMENTS _____

_____

_____

_____

_____

_____

If you think you are interested in a person, learn as much as you can about the person. You need to know if his name is Bob or Robert before you marry him; you need to know if her name is Cherry or Sherry before you marry her; and whatever you do, please learn to spell the name.

COMMENTS _____

_____

_____

_____

_____

_____

_____

_____

Learn as much as possible about their background, likes and dislikes, personality, family and family history, etc. You really do not want to get involved with the kind of person that would rather see you dead than to let you go.

COMMENTS _____

_____

_____

_____

_____

_____

List some other things you would want to know about the person?

_____
_____
_____
_____

Is this person dependable? Does this person keep their promises? Is this person timely or always late? Does this person consistently pull disappearing acts without excuses and avoids answering any questions that would clarify this behavior?

QUESTION: If you are considering a relationship, would the answers to these questions matter?

_____
_____
_____
_____
_____
_____

List your interests, likes and dislikes and make the same type of list for the other person. Below is an example:

<u>Your Interests and likes</u>

    Church

    Bike Riding

    Reading

    Going to the Movies

    Dancing

    Formal Affairs

    World Travel

<u>Your Dislikes</u>

    Beer

    Cigarettes, Cigars and Pipes

    Gambling

    Boating

<u>The Other Person's Interests and Likes</u>

    Hanging on the Corners

    Sitting on the Porch

    Laying on the Sofa

    Gambling Casinos

    Talking on the Phone

    Beer Drinking Contests

The Other Person's Dislikes

    Church

    Movies

    Dancing

    Reading

    Traveling

    Formal Affairs

Using the examples above, make lists of interests, likes and dislikes for yourself and the other person. Use a separate sheet of paper if needed.

Your Interests and Likes

1.

2.

3.

Your Dislikes

1.

2.

3.

The Other Person's Interests and Likes

1.

2.

3.

The Other Person's Dislikes

1.

2.

3.

QUESTION: Do you believe reading this book made a difference in how you responded to each item listed in this section?

_____
_____
_____
_____
_____
_____

If you are single and desire to be married, God has someone compatible for you. God did not give Adam the creatures, the fowl, the creeping things or fish for companionship because they were not compatible for him. God made what Adam needed and presented her to him. God made woman and Adam called her Eve and she was compatible for him. God will do the same for you. First of all, seek God and His will, be faithful to Him, be patient and content, and be confident in Him and in who you are in Him. Doing these things will prepare you to be a whole package.

About the Author

Sharon Lee Graham is a native of Chicago, Illinois. Her business career expands over a period of more than 37 years. She has a special interest in ministry. She has sat under teachings of some of the most profound Bible scholars and received her first license for ministry in 1966. She received her first public ordination to the ministry May 21, 1995, Chicago, Illinois. She has held the position of assistant pastor. In April 1997, she became the founder and pastor of Life In Christ~Christ In Me Ministries, Inc., and in April 2003, founder and president of Sharon Graham Ministries, Inc., in a Chicago western suburb.

In 2000, she was accepted into the Christian Satellite Bible University, Chicago, Illinois, where she majored in Christian Counseling. In 2001, she received her degree of Bachelor of Christian Education in Christian Counseling graduating class valedictorian, Summa Cum Laude; in 2002 she received her Master's Degree graduating Summa Cum Laude, and in 2004 she received her Doctoral Degree graduating Summa Cum Laude. The degrees were earned from the Christian Satellite Bible University, through the International Apostolic University of Grace and Truth, Indianapolis, Indiana (IAUGT). She continued her education and earned her Doctoral Degree in Theology from IAUGT in 2006 graduating Summa Cum Laude.

She loves to teach and is now writing books for publication. She is the sole proprietor of Dr. Sharon Lee Graham Productions, a company that produces written, visual and audio materials.

drslgproductions@sbcglobal.net

www.ingramcontent.com/pod-product-compliance
Lightning Source LLC
Chambersburg PA
CBHW071832290426
44109CB00017B/1804